WHAT HAPPENS WHEN YOU DIE

WRITTEN BY
TAMI BENZEL

THIS BOOK IS MY GIFT TO GOD. SO THAT ANYONE THAT READS THIS WILL REMEMBER THE GIFT THAT GOD HAS GIVEN US.

LIFE AND DEATH.

authorHOUSE™
1663 Liberty Drive, Suite 200
Bloomington, Indiana 47403
(800) 839-8640
www.AuthorHouse.com

First published by AuthorHouse 05/25/05

ISBN: 1-4208-3133-X (sc)

Printed in the United States of America
Bloomington, Indiana

This book is printed on acid-free paper.

Contents

CHAPTER ONE
THE ARRIVAL

Walking to the Church, I was amazed; I had never seen anything so magnificent, so large. It was as if you could put the whole world inside of it.

As I started walking up the stairs to enter the Church, a man was walking out with a large group of people, all with such peace on their faces. The man must have realized that I was confused about where I was.

"Hello." He said, "Can I help you?"

"Hi, I am not." Stumbling over my words "Not sure where I am."

"Well let me help you. This is where we come to worship God. I would stay here all day but there is much to do." He motioned for me to go ahead as he was saying. "Go in, worship God. And let him know how much you love him." With that, the man was off.

I am not sure how long I stayed there; it could have been two hours or two weeks. All I knew is this is where I wanted to be, Worshiping our Lord; I cannot put words to how it felt. More peace than I thought could exist.

I realized that there was a woman sitting beside me; I am not sure how long she had been there. It was like one moment nobody was there and the next moment she was. Humming a song that I knew.

"I know that song, I said," I sang it when I was a little girl."

"You must have just arrived."

"I don't know. --- I'm not real sure!" I stated

The woman giggled a little saying, "It will take you a while. And it's different here in heaven than on earth."

All of a sudden, I realized that I had died ---- O that day! , That day started flooding my head----And what about my family! "...

"How long have I been here!!!? What about my children? It's all coming back to me." I put my head in my hands shaking my head, not knowing what to do or think.

"It's ok dear." She said speaking very softly.

"But do you know how long I've been here!?"

"Well" She started to explain very happily, "I come three times a day, and you have been here about two weeks, Heaven time that is, Earth time you have been here two years."

"Two Years." I started to panic.!! "Two years--- what about my children!!? What about!!

She grabbed my hand saying, "It's alright dear-- Really God looks after your children, just like always."

My children were grown, both in their early twenty's, but the fact remained that they had never been without me. What they must be going through.

The lady suggested that I come home with her, get a bite to eat and I was hoping to get answers.

As we walked out of the church I looked around not really remembering the view that was before me, the roads, they really were paved with gold and the trees were so green that the color looked like it was falling off the tree on to the ground. It was so pretty. Even the paint on the houses was so beautiful it was as if the colors were talking to you.

I am sorry dear, I forgot to introduce myself, I am Hanna.

Walking to Hanna's, she greeted everybody with such love and warmth, and was greeted back the same. Hanna reminded me of the sweet grandmother; she looked as if she was in her fifty's, but had the pep of a thirty year old, you could tell her hair was long, but put up in a bun. Blackish gray hair. Very nice looking dark skin. She was dressed in a long flowing summer dress. Dressed for the perfect summer day.

"Hanna." I asked, "Do you know everybody?"

"Of course dear, we are all Gods children."

"I see, are you like the welcome wagon?"

"We all are dear."

We came to the cutest little cottage, I turned back and realized we were out in the country and we had not walked that far, but not even the hint of a town was near.

"Hanna how long have we been walking?"

"Not long dear, why?" she asked

"Well, where did the town go?

Not really getting the answer I was looking for Hanna simply said I live in the country.

"Please come in." Hanna invited.

We came through the side door into the kitchen. It looked just like you would expect a kitchen in a cute little cottage to look. At the same time, I have to say it was a lot bigger than it looked from the outside.

"Are you tired, would you like to rest?" Hanna asked

"I'm not sure, but I would rather stay awake, I spent two weeks, really two years and didn't know it. What if I slept for a hundred years?"

"That won't happen." Hanna said with a chuckle

Hanna set a glass of tea in front of me, and it was the best tea I have ever tasted.

"What kind of tea is this Hanna?"

"Just tea, but you will find that everything in heaven is better than you have ever tasted, even the water tastes different."

As I sat there so many questions was going though my mind. Hanna came over, sat down with me, and started telling me things about heaven.

"There is no crime, nothing that is bad, no jealousy, no fear. You can sleep out under the stars and have no fear. Everything is at total peace, can you feel it?"

"Yes I can, especially at church, I didn't want to leave."

"We all love to be in church, but that peace you feel is everywhere, the reason you feel it more there is because there are so many souls in one place worshipping God."

"I see."

I remember when I first got here. I asked for paper and ink, I didn't want to forget a thing." Hanna explained.

"How long have you been here Hanna?"

"Well." Hanna stared up as to try to remember. "I'm not sure, do you remember what year it was when you left?"

"It was two thousand three."

"I think it was the year 1813, almost 200 years ago, give or take ten years and there has not been one sad moment since, its been paradise." she said with a smile.

I looked at her odd and Hanna just giggled saying it would come to me.

"Is there only one church in town or are there more?"

"There's only one church anywhere, everybody goes to the same one, where or why dear would you think there would be more than one, after all there is only one God, doesn't that make sense to you."

"Yes it does, earth would probably be a better place if we all had just one church."

Before I knew it, we had eaten and Hanna had invited me to freshen up before we headed back to church, change my clothes if I desired.

"That's very kind of you but I don't have any other clothes."

"That's not a problem dear, the changing room is at the top of the stairs, and would you like a summer dress?"

"Yes a summer dress would be nice, if it's no problem."

"Its no problem at all, go on up and help yourself, you will find everything you need." said Hanna

Oddly enough, there was a summer dress and everything I needed.

Coming down the stairs, I was asking how she did that but she just said later dear.

As we were walking to church, I was getting excited about getting back to church near our Lord, I also wanted to pay attention to see how far we walked, but before I knew it, we were back in town and Hanna's place was gone.

Back at church there was a man talking about how great God is. Several other men got up and spoke. The church was always full of family's of all ages.

"Hanna where's God?" I asked

"He's everywhere." Hanna went on to say "what a wonderful place he has made for us, and the love he has for all of us."

"I know, it's almost breathtaking, I never want to leave here, it makes you wonder why we stay on earth or scared to die, but I do miss my children."

"Don't worry about that, God looks out for them just as he always has."

After church, we walked out and I realized I do not know where to go.

"Hanna." I asked, "You have been very kind to me and well, I don't mean to impose, but I have no where to stay."

"Come with me, we will get a bite to eat."

We came to a beautiful huge hotel. The building was so tall you could not see the top of it.

"Hanna, we have a hotel in heaven?"

"Sure dear, we have everything, and there is a great place to eat in here also, and that's what we are going to do, eat.

"Do we need money?" I asked.

"Money, what's money?"

"On earth its how you got a meal, your home, clothes, everything that you want, you have to have money."

"And what does this money look like?"

"Its green paper, or silver coins." I explained

"Green paper, how strange."

That was the end of our money talk.

Inside the hotel was so lovely. Just as warm and friendly, it was done in marble that brought a very elegant look, there were plenty of places to sit and visit with people.

A man came over grabbing Hanna's hands greeting us.

"Hanna good to see you, what can I do for you and your friend?"

"We would like to get a bite to eat."

The man turns to me saying, "Are you enjoying heaven?"

"Yes but I haven't been here that long, only for a couple of weeks." I said

"Well once you are here you will not want to leave, I assure you. Now follow me ladies. I will seat you in the dinning area."

Walking in the dinning room area was so pretty and just as elegant, on earth you would have to be very wealthy to enjoy this, it had huge chandeliers that lit the whole room, soft music playing and the table cloths were so white they almost glowed; even the forks had a shine I had never seen before.

A waiter came over to the table.

"Hello ladies it's good to see you, what can I get you?"

"What do you have?" I asked

"We have everything, anything you want my lady."

"Pasta, that sounds good."

"Maybe thee would like some fresh greens with that?" He asked "And a stern of tea?

"Yes that would be nice, but I only want a glass --- of tea," I said, thinking a stern of tea would be way too much. But-----I was hungry and didn't realize it until we sat down and I started thinking of what I want.

"And for you Hanna, what can I get for you my lady?" and he bowed as if he was in the presence of royalty.

"The same kind sir."

"I will have your food up in moments." and the man bowed and walked away.

The restaurant was full of people coming and going. Laughing, praying, and eating.

"In heaven its not where you lived on earth it's what century did you get here. There are souls here from the 1500's, 1600's, later than that, it's always fun to try to guess, but you can tell sometimes by the way they talk, the words they use." explained Hanna

"And we have jobs here Hanna?" I asked

"Yes, but not like you think. The man waiting on us is here because he wants to be here. Now we might not see him again here. Or he might decide to stay for a while. It's up to him what he wants to do, because let me tell you there is a lot to do here in heaven."

"But what happens if nobody wants to do this?"

Hanna looked at me in an odd way saying, "I don't know, that's never happened, but do you understand."

"I think so, so what other kind of jobs are there in heaven?"

"There are no stress jobs, no jobs you don't want to go to. The times I did visit earth, people always complained about their jobs, its not like that here, this is truly paradise."

After a wonderful meal, it was time to go and I was a little worried about what to do next. Where I was going to stay? I guess I could go back to church. I stayed there two weeks.

"Hanna, you have been very kind to me, but I have no place to stay."

"Dear maybe you should stay here, in the hotel."

That sounded good to me. Get my thoughts together; try to go over the past couple of weeks. Hanna stayed with me till the man came for me to take me up to my room.

"Thank you Hanna for everything. Will I see you again?" I asked

"Of course dear, I will see you in church and you know where I live."

And with that, Hanna gave me a hug and as she walked away, I realized I don't really know where she lives.

"Are you ready?" the man asked

"Yes,--yes I am thank you." I said

In the room, it was like a dream. It was or it looked like a penthouse, with flowers all around, and beautiful furniture. I opened double doors and there was my bedroom, with a large canopy bed, the sheets were already down, ready for me and even the bathroom was large and elegant with a huge hot tub that was already filled with hot silky water,

After a long and much needed bath, there was a robe waiting for me. I lay down on the bed without even getting under the sheets and that's the last thing I remember till I heard a knock on the door.

CHAPTER TWO
MEETING WITH THE HIGHER COUNSELORS

When I opened the door there was a young lady standing there with a very beautiful smile and very happy, you could feel her joy. She was very attractive; she has long flowing brown hair. A beautiful flowered dress on, with sandal's, which looked as if they had come out of the first century, but the dress looked like today's style.

"Good morning. Did you sleep well? She asked

"Fine thank, you."

It was as if I knew her and could not figure out where I had seen her or met her before. She started to laugh saying "I know it's all new to you, but I thought I would walk to church with you, if that is all right with you?"

"That would be nice, but I need to shower and get dressed."

"Great, then I will be downstairs in the lobby waiting for you. I almost forgot, I'm Claudia, it's good to see you."

After she left I hurried so as not to keep her waiting to long. I opened the closet door, there was a dress waiting for me, and it was a perfect fit. Just like at Hanna's.

Walking to church, Claudia and I did not say too much. She was greeting everybody and stopping to talk to people along the way.

Walking up to the church, I am still amazed how magnificent it was.

Claudia stopped to talk to some more people that were walking out of church. I stood back and watched all the people coming and going. They all looked like they were filled with peace and happiness. Happy to be going, and a great feeling when they left. I was excited about going in myself that without even realizing it I had a big smile on my face thanking God I could enter such a place.

After we left church Claudia asked if I would go somewhere with her. And well, since my day was wide open I agreed...

As we walked, Claudia explained where we were going, and whom we were going to meet with. She assured me that some of my questions would be answered. And that was what I wanted was my questions to be answered.

We came to a big building that reminded me of an old courthouse that had been restored. Inside the building looked like the outside, old but very beautiful, a lot of woodwork on the walls that looked like it was done 100's of years ago but kept like it was built yesterday. We came to double doors and Claudia opened them up.

"This is as far as I go; I will be waiting for you here. It will be fine. These men are here to help you, not judging you or telling you what to do; they are here to guide you."

I was feeling a little nervous.

Walking in the room it looked like the last supper. There were five men at a long table all facing me, they all had rather long beards, with white robes and they appeared very stern. This room looked different than the rest of the building, well what I had seen of it anyway. It was all done in marble that started on the floor and the design went all the way up on the ceiling.

The middleman motioned for me to sit in the chair that was in front of them, I kind of felt as if I was on trial. One of the men must have realized that and let me know that everything was fine. The man in the middle was the first to ask me a question.

"Do you remember when you got here?"

"No, I mean I'm not sure."

"What do you remember?" another man asked

"I was standing in front of the church, and then I went in, and the next thing I remember is meeting Hanna."

"The church, its beautiful is it not."

"Yes, like I've never seen before." I said

This got a smile out of them, and then the middleman spoke again

"All right Sarah."

Sarah , that is my name, how funny that I did not remember that, or had not even thought about it.

"What would you like to know?"

"What about my children? I've been gone for a couple of years, well earth time."

"They're fine. God watches out for them, they are fine Sarah. But they are waiting for a sign from you as on earth they do when a loved one leaves."

"How do I see them?' I asked, I started to get a little excited about this "And when? ----"

The forth man spoke " the first couple of times we would like to send Claudia with you, show you how to get there and back , but you must understand that there are rules to them you have passed."

I started nodding my head as if I understood.

The fifth man spoke "are you enjoying heaven so far?"

"Yes, very much, but where should I stay?" I asked

"Stay at the hotel for now, till things clear up for you, we'll talk about that another time."

The man at the end of the table asked "Sarah when you were on earth where did you want to live?"

"Well it was different, sometimes it was by the ocean, and then I would dream of living in a field of flowers as far as the eye can see."

"Then keep that in mind."

"But where ever I live I want to be near the church." I said

"Yes we understand, but no matter where you live you will always be in walking distance of the church."

"Yes." another man spoke "Remember when you were at Hanna's, she lives out in the country but she is still in walking distance to the church and town."

With that the middleman stood up "it was nice of you to come see us Sarah; we will see you again soon."

I guess that was my cue to leave. As I stood up, I was not sure if I should shake their hands, bow, or just excuse myself. I chose half a bow and excused myself. Walking out of the room Claudia was waiting with such excitement as if she knew what they had been saying in the room and maybe she did.

"All right Sarah what would you like to do first?"

"Go see my children."

"We will in good time, but first lets head back to church, then get a bite to eat. Is the food great here or what?" Claudia asked.

"I haven't had much of it, but I have enjoyed it."

After church and a bite to eat, Claudia suggested that we take a walk out in the country.

"Do you want to go horse back riding Sarah?" Claudia asked.

"Yes, I would, when I was a little girl my aunt and I would go riding all the time, I always had a good time."

"I remember that," said Claudia.

I looked at her very strange asking her "what do you mean you remember that?"

"We are family Sarah; I was already here when you were born. I have always come in and out to check on you. I go see everybody in our family. There is a lot of family too. But I am your cousin, now I don't know if I'm your 5th cousin or your 15th, but it doesn't really matter, because no matter what we are family and I am so glad you are here."

I started getting excited "Claudia." I asked, "I have a brother that died years ago."

"Yes Greg, he's here. We will see him; we want to ease you into this because there is a lot to take in. He knows you are here, and he will also help you along the way."

I was thinking that at first with all the new faces and new places, I was feeling a little lonely, well unless I was at church. It was as if I knew everybody but could not remember anyone. However, I am so thankful to be here.

"When do I get to see my brother?" I asked.

"Tomorrow, we are going to have a family reunion see." Claudia started to explain, "When we die, or well I don't really like to use that term. The only thing that dies is your body you had on earth. However, sometimes when they come as fast as you did, souls are not ready for all of this or they stay behind. That can be very sad because nobody can see them. However, as I said, when they do come home as fast as you did we do not want to rush you. God says eternity------ therefore it means we have plenty of time. But I have to say you are doing very well."

I felt a little proud of this, although in heaven it was not hard.

We were walking as we talked and before I knew it, we were out in the middle of a pasture. That was going to take me a while to get used to. One minute you are in town and 5 minutes later, you are in the middle of the country. It's as if you are 100's of miles away from anything.

In the middle of the pasture stood a man with two horses: they were saddled and ready to go. Claudia greeted and thanked the man and he left just over the hill.

"Claudia." I asked after we mounted the horses "how did that man know we were coming?"

Claudia just laughed, not giving me an answer she asked, "where to, the ocean or."

Before she could suggest anything else, I agreed that the ocean would be the place to see.

"All right then, the ocean it is."

It did not take long and we were standing in front of the ocean, (it was just over the hill). The view was so great, I stopped my horse to take it all in; I could see the most beautiful white sandy beaches. The water was so clear and blue that you could see the bottom of the oceans floor for miles. Well, as far as the eye could see. It was breathtaking.

"I could stay here forever." I said in a daze.

"Remember what the counselors told you about where you want to live. There are so many beautiful places here and you have only seen a very, very small part of it. I am so excited. No matter how long I have been here, you never tire of this, its still such a wonder. You never get over the power of our Lord and what he has created for all of us."

"I could stay here forever." I said.

After spending time riding the horses and swimming in the ocean, it was time to get back. I was ready. Claudia got off her horse, tied the bridle to the saddle, and said goodbye and even thanked the horse for an enjoyable ride and let it go, as the horse went back the way we came.

"Claudia shouldn't we take them back, what if they get lost?" I asked.

"They know the way Sarah, its fine, but you need to do the same so they can go together."

"All right, but that seems odd to me."

"They go over the hill. The man that was there takes care of them. He loves his animals. Anyway they go right back to their ranch she explained."

Back at church, everyone seems so happy to be there. The children listened with such enthusiasm. And after church, everybody goes outside to talk and tell each other what has been going on in their lives. They all have such peace on their face. The children are running and playing and nobody getting hurt, no children fighting, it was wonderful to see this.

"What are you doing?" Claudia asked.

"I'm just watching everybody. They are so happy."

"Of course they are silly, we're in heaven."

"Yes we are." I said and I realized this is where I wanted to be, in heaven, near God.

Claudia and I walked to the hotel and got a bite to eat and then it was time to rest. I thanked her for a great day.

"Will I see you tomorrow?" I asked.

"Yes, remember after church we are going to see the rest of the family."

I was excited, I have only lost about four people in my life and tomorrow I will be seeing them again, plus people I never met before that is family.

Walking into my room, I had already forgotten how nice the room was. I wondered if all the rooms were this nice. I opened the curtains and could not believe my eyes. There were billions and billions of stars and I am not sure but I thought I could see earth and several other planets. I did not really know what floor I was on. There are no buttons on the elevator, but there is a man on there that takes you to the right floor and walks you to your room, but I was pretty high up, it was like I was closer to outer space then the ground due to the fact when I looked down it was hard to see ground.

I decided to take a hot bath and go to bed, only this time I got under the sheets and slept so well. When I woke, I felt so rested. I never rested like this on earth; I don't believe anybody on earth rests until they come home.

CHAPTER THREE
THE FAMILY REUNION

In the morning, Claudia was there early and I was ready this time.

"Good morning Claudia, how was your evening?" I asked.

"It was great. I went to earth to check in on family and I think we are going to have more company."

"What do you mean?"

"Somebody in our family is getting ready to come home. I don't think we know till they get here. Only God can choose that. There might be more for them to do on earth. God has a purpose for all of us, to help other people or ourselves."

I was listening to her, realizing that on earth this would be a very sad time, but here in heaven we rejoice our family coming home. If we only knew what was waiting for us. I guess we do. It's all in the bible. However, sometimes on earth, it is hard to see what is ahead. I guess that's where faith comes in. But being here, you realize how many miracles we have on earth and do not even know it.

After church, we started walking out of town.

"Where are we going Claudia?" I asked.

"To the family reunion, everybody is waiting for us."

As we walked, I realized we were almost to Hanna's.

"Are we going to Hanna's? " I asked.

"Yes we are. Hanna is also part of the family. She is like your sixth or seventh grandmother; I do not really know how far it goes back. However, as I said before it does not really matter. We are all family. We are all God's children..."Why didn't she say anything?"

"Because we didn't want to rush you, it can be very overwhelming .We are here, this is going to be so much fun, I'm so excited."

Walking into Hanna's I saw my grandpa standing with a few other men. They were talking about the jobs they have taken on since they have been in heaven and how joyful their lives are.

"My grandpa looked up over at me with a big smile saying, "Well look who's here. We've been waiting for you."

It was a little shocking seeing him, after all the last time I saw him was at his funeral.

He came over, gave me a hug, and then led me around the room to meet everyone. It was a wonderful time meeting everybody, but the best thing so far was meeting his parents. I was starting to understand taking it slow, it could be overwhelming.

Claudia came up behind me grabbing me by the elbow leading me away as she excused us.

"Didn't I tell you this was going to be fun, but there is somebody waiting for you in the kitchen. He just got here."

Walking into the kitchen stood my brother. I almost fell to the floor, I started crying uncontrollably, I went over and hugged him so tight, I did not want to let go.

"Its ok now, we are together again, and I missed you," he said.

"I missed you so much to-------."

When I finally stopped crying, we sat at the kitchen table and talked about everything under the sun. I told him that Claudia said that someone else was getting ready to come home, but she never said whom it was. We talked about my children and their children.

"The family has really grown, everybody's grandparents now, but as you see, the family is large. Anyway, how have you been enjoying heaven so far? Do you have any questions that I have not answered? " Greg asked.

"Yes I do have a question, after you had been gone about 5 years, I had a dream and in that dream, you came to me, asked if I was ok, and let me know you were alright. Was that a dream or did you really come to me?"

"Yes I really came to you, you seemed to be having a hard time, but as you see I had only been here for about 5 weeks. I was exploring everything. You will see Claudia and I will show you."

We sat for a long time talking and everybody that walked in the kitchen, if I had not met them before, would come over and tell me who they were. Even though I had just met most of these people, I knew they really loved me. It is hard to explain, you can feel it, but no matter what time period they came from, they all had the same goal, to be near and worship God and do his work.

We all gathered outside in Hanna's back yard, it was so pretty, it had so many tall trees and the leaves were so green. She had a short white fence around the yard, that way you could still see the forest behind her house. There were flowers all the way around, lining the fence. She even had a garden. There were several picnic tables that were full of food, anything you would want. We all took our places and joined hands. One of the uncles started praying, thanking God for everything around us, thanking God for his love, they even thanked God for me. It was truly a good day to be in heaven.

After we all ate, we visited more. The children that were there were running around the yard playing. I did not know how long they were here but I would guess they were here before I was born. They were all having such fun. At the end of the day, we all decided to gather at the church. Everybody always likes to end every day in church. Walking to the church, I realized we were a huge group. However, no matter how many people showed up in church it was always big enough for thousands of people at one time.

Several of the men that were in our group got up and spoke, even my brother. I felt so proud. He gave thanks to Jesus for dying on the cross so that we could enjoy this paradise. We were all filled with the holy sprit. We all stood up and raised our hands as far as we could to our Lord. It was so satisfying to be there and let the Lord know that we loved Him and worshiped Him.

After church, I finally got the chance to talk to Hanna and thank her for all she has done for me. We all said our goodbyes and after everybody went their own way, the only ones that were left were Claudia, Greg and myself.

"Well." I said feeling happier than I could remember, "I think we should get a snack at the hotel I'm staying at."

"Great idea." They both agreed at the same time.

As we were eating, Greg suggested that we walk to the top of the mountain and look at the stars.

"I remember when I was a little girl you and I would get up real early and ride our bikes to the end of the street, all you could see was pasture from there and when the sun came up it was so beautiful ."

"Yes I remember that" he said.

It was nice that he remembered some things about our childhood. Being here it was easy to forget some things. I had not realized this but

I have not thought about my family that was still on earth all day. I was having so much fun here.

We went walking in the country. It was night but between the stars and the moon, it lit the way. We started walking up the hill, climbed some rocks, and before I knew it, we were standing on top of the mountain. Looking over, it was unbelievable!!!! It was as if it was a picture, but way too great too have ever been painted. You could see into the depths of the universe and gaze into the valleys of everything God had created. ----------- It was spectacular. Heaven seemed to be right in the middle of all the planets known to man and then some, so many stars. We all laid down and looked up at the many wonders of heaven. We all laid there not saying a word until finally my brother broke the silence asking.

"What do you think Sarah?"

"I don't believe there are words to sum it up."

Claudia laughed saying "no matter how many times I see this, wow sum's it up."

We all stayed until morning talking about everything, me asking question after question. But when the sun came up, I was breathless. Never had I seen such a sunrise as in heaven. It looked so close you could touch it. It never got any hotter. As a matter fact, the weather has been perfect here everyday, never to hot never to cold, just perfect.

"Does it ever snow or rain here?" I asked.

"Sure if you want it to. Just ask God." Greg said.

We all stood there the rest of the time watching the sun finish rising. It was time to get back. My brother was standing beside me and hugged me, telling me how great it was to have me home.

As we walked back to town to get ready for church, Claudia went over some of the things we were going to do today.

"It's almost time to go see your children. There are some things you need to understand, so we are going back to see the counselors. They will explain everything to you that you need to know."

"They are very smart men." Greg said, "We all listen to them, after all they get all their answers and information from God himself.

CHAPTER FOUR
GOING BACK HOME

After church, my brother excused himself.

"Where are you going?" I asked

"I have some things to do, plus I thought even as nice as the hotel is, you might like to stay with me."

"That would be great. ~~~ I would really like that."

"Good than I will get things ready."

Then Claudia and I stood. We need to go see the counselors, they are waiting for us." said Claudia.

Sitting in front of the counselors once again, the middleman spoke first.

"So things are coming together for you?"

"Yes thank you sir. I have met a lot of my family."

The second man spoke.

"It's truly a wonder is it not?"

"Yes sir it is, what I have seen."

"And no matter how long you are here; if it's a week or a thousand years it will always be a wonder."

I was thinking that he was talking from experience.

The first man spoke again.

"You are going to visit your children? We told you the first meeting that there are rules. We must make sure that you understand this. It has been a couple of years since you have been there and they are waiting for something from you."

I nodded my head to agree as he still spoke.

"You cannot interfere with their lives. You can only watch and prepare their place in heaven as your family has done for you."

"They are all right?" I asked

"Yes." another man spoke." They are fine. But remember that on earth you were there to guide them. You can not do that now."

"I understand. But how will they know I'm there or that I've come to see them?"

"You can watch them for a while. You can stay for days, that is up to you. But as you see in heaven, it's always good to be here. It's nice to check in on them. And to let them know that you have been there, you can always go to them in their dreams. Claudia can show you the way to do that in time."

The man at the end of the table spoke up.

Did Hanna explain earth time to you?"

"Yes she said two weeks in heaven was two years on earth."

"That is correct. So you see it really won't be that long before you are all together again."

I sat there not sure how I felt about that.

Then the man at the end spoke.

"So, you are going to stay with your brother?"

"Yes sir."

"That's good. He is very good about showing the way also, as is Claudia. Soon you can think about getting your own place. But there is no hurry."

"Thank you sirs."

The middle man started to speak again.

"The first several times you go see your family, Claudia will go. She will show you the way.

I shook my head and stood up to excuse myself, and like before, I gave a half bow.

Claudia was standing outside of the room waiting for me.

"Are you ready to go see the children?" Claudia asked.

"What ~~~ now" I asked.

"Yes silly. But if you're not ready, we can wait awhile. There is nothing saying we have to go know."

"No, I want to go. You will stay with me while I'm there won't you?" I asked

"Yes Sarah. I won't leave. I will stay by your side. It will be fine. Don't worry." Claudia assured.

"Alright but before we go, lets go back to church. Pray about it." I suggested.

"That's a wonderful idea. We will get everybody to pray with us."

When we got to church, Claudia stood up and told everybody about our journey. We didn't even have to ask people to pray with us. They all stood up and we all prayed together that I have a safe and great visit. They also prayed for a safe trip home. That was kind of strange; I was thinking why wouldn't we have a safe trip back?

After saying our goodbyes to everyone Claudia suggested we go.

"Are you ready Sarah?"

"Right now I'm a little nervous. I don't know why, but I am."

"Would you care to wait? It's up to you." Claudia asked.

"No ~~ I'm ready."

"Great~~" Claudia said as she started explaining that she had been there and there were some changes. But good ones. What I didn't realize is that as she was talking, we were on our way. Then all of a sudden, we were standing in what use to be my living room.

There has been change's. Everything looked great. I went over to where all the pictures where hanging and realized that the furniture was not the only thing that had changed. There were people in the picture I had never seen before. A man and a baby girl.

"Claudia, did my daughter have another child?"

"Yes. She got married about six months after you came home. And then a year later she had Rosés."

"Roses~~ what a wonderful name." I said as I started to cry.

Claudia came over and put her arm around me saying. "It's alright Sarah; this is why we try to prepare you. Nothing stays the same, everybody and everything changes. That's good Sarah. Changes are good. Your daughter has a new baby. A husband that loves her, He also loves her first child."

As Claudia was talking, all of a sudden the front door opened and in walked my oldest daughter with the two kids. She sat the baby down in a baby's chair and started supper. "Claudia." I whispered as if they could hear me." "Can Roses see us?"

Claudia laughed at the fact that I was whispering.

"Don't worry they can't hear or see us. Well the baby can. She will lose that as she gets older. But right know we can play with her. Look Sarah, she's smiling at you."

"I was always told that when a baby smiles it's because the angels are playing with her."

"Well angels or family. Sometimes both." said Claudia as she was making faces at the baby.

We stayed for a while watching my daughter taking such loving care of the two kids. She was still fixing dinner when the front door opened again. It was her husband. He came in, talked to both of the children, and made his way over to kiss my daughter.

"How was your day?" he asked

"Good and yours?"

"It was fine. But it's nice to be home."

As they sat down to eat, my other daughter came in.

"Hi. Hey, it looks like I'm in time for dinner she said with a laugh.

"Have a seat" they offered.

"No I'm kidding. I have to get home. I wanted to see if taking the kids Saturday was still good."

"How about if you take Bennie. The baby might be too much." said my oldest daughter. "That's fine. I better get going. I'll be back Saturday for you Bennie. Be ready for a good time buddy."

"Claudia, she doesn't live here in my house to." I asked

"Not your house Sarah, their house, and this works for them. Your oldest daughter has a family. That wouldn't work for somebody that has a career."

"I see. I'm ready to go Claudia."

"I understand. It's hard the first time, to think that their lives have gone on without you."

"I missed her wedding and the birth of her second child. I don't even know what her husband's name is."

"His name is Brad." Claudia tried to comfort me "and he loves your daughter and the two kids very much."

"What about my other daughter, is she married?

"Not yet. It's not time for her. God has a plan for her and that's what she's working on. It's very important to her. Sarah you raised good strong women. Be proud of them. God is."

"He is." I said as I dried my eyes.

"Yes, and he's proud of you and me. He is so forgiving, that when we do come up short of His grace, he picks us back up He loves us so much, and heaven proves that."

I stood there not really knowing how I felt about any of this.

"Would you like to go now Sarah?" Claudia asked.

"Yes I'm ready." I said sadly.

"Great, this is going to be fun. I have been so excited to show you this."

I could see and hear the excitement in Claudia.

"Let's step out side Sarah ~~ we are going to take the long ~~ way home."

After stepping outside, we were suddenly floating in the air. I looked down and could see for miles and miles. I could see the planes coming in and landing.

"This is so cool Claudia." I said.

"I thought you would enjoy this. It's one of my favorite things to do. This is what I do when you are talking with the higher counselors."

"Really, and I thought you were patiently waiting..."

Claudia just laughs as we kept getting higher and higher. Before I knew it, we were surrounded by blackness from space and billions of stars. I was thinking to myself ~~ this is where all the stars are. On earth the only way to see this many stars at one time, is to be exactly where I am right now.

"Can we stay here for awhile? It's beautiful here." I asked.

"Yes we can. I thought you would enjoy this."

And then Claudia started to explain what was going on weather wise on earth.

"Look Sarah, over there in the middle, it looks like there's a snowstorm going on, but over on this side it looks to be sunny and warm. From here it looks so big and peaceful."

"I feel like the luckiest soul alive." I commented.

After staying there for a while, we both felt the need to get back to church and let everybody know that we were back and things went as fine as I guess they could.

Church was great. Everyone seemed so delighted to know that we had a good trip and were back home.

After church, Claudia asked me if I was ok.

I said yes, but hesitated for a second or two.

"The first couple of times are really hard for most people. But once you have been here for a while, it gets easier, especially since you know what's ahead for them. Claudia said.

"Yes, your right, words can't explain how amazing heaven really is."

"Besides, we have a universe to explore. It's a big place. And we are going to have a great time seeing everything. And there are ways to talk to your children. Remember when your brother came to you in your dreams? Even you said that it made you feel better. " Claudia explained.

"Yes your right again. However, I really have to admit that I love being here so much, near God that I would not want to go back. I guess I'm feeling a little bad about that."

"What!!!. Don't feel bad!!. Everyone gets to enjoy heaven at one time or another. Sarah I was so happy when I heard you were coming home. Some day your children will come home also. I think before we go to them in their dreams, we should probably go visit a few more times. That way we can be very positive about the visit. Because remember we cannot change their path.

Did you know that we all have someone we look out for? And even though we look after someone on earth, we can still not interfere. Do you know who I looked after Sarah?"

"Who? I asked.

"You Sarah, I watched over you. Claudia said with a warm smile.

"Really and how did that go for you?" I said jokingly.

"Well you were difficult at times but now that you are here; we are going to have a great time. All my friends have been asking about you. I can't wait till they meet you."

CHAPTER FIVE
OUT ON THE OCEAN

The walk to church this morning was absolutely wonderful. The sun was shining as it always does. And as I walked by the house's even the grass and trees seemed to be saying good morning. What a great feeling it was to be here among all the beautiful colors of heaven. It looked like a canvas that you would only see in a painting. Because nowhere else could such a beautiful picture lie.

I met up with Claudia and my brother at the church doors. After we all greeted one another we went in to take our seats. As we sat down, I realized that there were more people than normal. There was always a lot of people, church never ended. So people come and go all day and night. Today it's as if everyone decided to come at the same time. Now heaven doesn't seem to end, it goes as far as the mind can imagine and then some. So I can't even think how many souls are here in the same place this very moment. I also didn't realize that my brother had not sat down with us.

When my brother did return, I could see the excitement on his face.

"You guys are never going to believe who came home today." He said

"Who?" Claudia and I asked at the same time.

Now I have only been here about three or four weeks, so I had no idea what all the commotion was about.

"Look Sarah. He's finely home."

"Who you guys. I can't see. Is it someone we know?" I asked

"No." My brother started to explain as everybody greeted the man as he made his way to the front of the church. "He lived his whole life for

God. He was all over the earth telling people how to come to God. That God would save them from any harm."

"Yes Sarah, that big house that you passed, well it's like a mansion. God made it himself for the man. They say he never strayed from the word of God. You know how hard that is on earth. And he's home now, what a blessed day it is." Claudia said as tears of joy rolled down her face.

The man started to talk. He told us about his experience on earth spreading the word of God to all four corners of the earth. He said he saw a lot. His life was always filled with joy no matter where he was.

After church we all waited to shake the man's hand and welcome him home personally. Then it was off to my Brother Greg's house.

"Did you go see the girls?" Greg asked.

"Yes." I said.

"Things have changed a little since she was home. I think it was a little hard for her." Claudia explained.

"Yes I remember it was hard for me also. Mom had gotten very sick. I was visiting her one time shortly after I had come home. She was having a hard time getting up the stairs, so I came up behind her and helped her the rest of the way." Greg said.

I looked at him strangely saying. "I thought we could not interfere?"

"That was really not interfering. I was just helping her. She was very sick. Besides I'm not even sure that she knew it was me."

"She did know. I know this because she told me. She said she felt someone come up behind her and help her. She said it was you. ~~~" I said with excitement in my voice.

"Well she was right." He said and they both hugged me laughing.

"Don't worry you will get all of this in time." Claudia said.

"I still have a lot to learn." But as I said this, I was thinking how I could let the children know I'm still here, watching over them.

Once again we came to the ocean where my brother's beautiful boat glistened in the sun light with every wave that came in.

"Here we are. I have your room ready. I'm so excited about you staying with me. I like to sail the ocean, I think you'll like it to."

"I didn't realize that you liked the ocean also." I said.

"I love it. I thought we would all go sailing. The stars on the mountain are really beautiful but on the ocean they are so bright that they look like they are coming from the sky and the ocean. It's also nice to sit back and watch all the things swimming in the ocean. We can even swim with them. Getting on the boat, I realized this was not just a small boat. It was huge and so elegant; my brother took me down to my room. I couldn't believe the size.

"Greg this is so nice. Have you always lived here, since you have been in heaven?

"No, well when I first got here, I stayed in the hotel for awhile and then I stayed with Hanna till I moved out here. I've been here ever since. It's so pretty out here. I love the ocean smells and the whales and, and well everything. You'll see for yourself..."

We ate on the deck while the boat was still docked at shore. Before we took the boat out in the middle of the ocean, night was coming on. The moon shines so bright that even with the night sky you can still see everything. We got out real far being we could not see land anymore. My brother had chairs that reclined back and we all sat there enjoying all the stars and watching all the sea creatures... With the boat going in a swaying movement.

"This is so relaxing," said Claudia.

"Everything is relaxing here in heaven."

"There are so many shooting stars, you never see this on earth." I commented.

"That's because they are souls coming home."

"There are so many at one time, and there is somebody for everybody, that's amazing."

After sitting there, watching everybody coming home, my brother decided to take a swim.

"Come on you guys. Want to go swimming? The dolphins are here. They can take you far down to see what's on the bottom, said Greg"

"Well I think that's my ride back. I need to get home, said Claudia"

"Come to think of it Claudia, I don't know were you live, I said"

Jokingly, she said, "just over the hill." I live in town; we have been so busy with showing you everything that I forgot all about that. I am not there much. Once in awhile I stay there for the day. The only place I go is church. We will go to my place tomorrow

"Sounds great." I said

With that, Claudia jumped in the water saying her goodbyes.

"What are you doing?" I asked

My brother laughed a little "she's going back to shore. "

"Should we take her? "

"No" said Claudia. "I do this all the time. Some of the dolphins swim with me so if I get tired they jump in there and help me out. Its fun, you should try it sometime. "

"I will" I said as Claudia swam away. Then it left my brother and myself. Heaven is so heavenly "I said".

"Yes and just when you think it can't get any better it does. I tell you the Lord is so good to us. There is nothing bad here. It is as God promised us and more."

We spent the night out in the middle of the ocean. My bed was so comfortable. So many pillows and the smell's were so good. There were flowers in a vase, I wondered with all the swaying how they stayed but they did.

Morning came and I got up and got ready for church. When I went on deck we were already back at shore...

"Good morning." said Greg with a big smile.

"Good morning. When did you bring us back to shore?"

I could tell we had been there for a while; the table on the deck was set for two. With pancakes, sausage, bacon, anything you wanted.

"Wow, did you do all this? What a wonderful spread."

"We have only been docked for an hour or so, and breakfast, well I wanted to make something special for you. Please sit down; would you like some coffee, or orange juice or both".

"Both." I said with excitement.

The meal was great; we cleaned up and headed to church.

After church Claudia took me to see her place, it was an older looking colonial house, beautiful landscape; the house was done in what looked like old furniture that was kept very well.

"Very nice, you live here by yourself?" I asked

"Well I always like to let anybody stay here. Sometimes souls don't want their own place they are so busy that they either stay in the hotel or here. So I let the souls at the hotels know that it's open for anybody that wants to be here. One time this man stayed for several years. Took care of all the other people that stayed, you know cooked for everybody. He loved to take care of the yard work. He always said that when he was on earth he could not keep plants alive but here he had a green thumb. He finally realized that everything in heaven grows with little effort on our part, but he still enjoyed it".

After spending time at Claudia's we met my brother back at church and had decided to go visit our mother, who was still living on earth. With all the new things here and visiting my children, I had not realized I could go see them. I did know I just had been so wrapped up with everything else. We also checked in to see the children.

CHAPTER SIX
TALKING TO THE CHILDREN

I had decided today that I would go see the children alone. Claudia and I had spent many times there and I felt that I was ready and could get back just fine.

"Good morning" I said as my brother walked on the deck.

My brother was just getting up and I had breakfast ready for him this morning

"Well look at you, breakfast for me, how very nice. Thank you."

"You are most welcome," I said

"I have decided to go see the children alone today. What do you think?" I asked

"I think you and I should go see the counselors before you do that"

"Why" I asked

"Because they can advise you on what's best, after all they do get all their guidance from God himself."

"Yes you are right, can we go after church?" I asked

"Sure we can, and we can see if Claudia wants to go also."

When we got to the counselors just like the other times they were waiting for me. It was so funny that you never see them at church. Although the church is always open, and I guess with them being like Gods right hand they wouldn't be there a lot.

The middleman nodded for me to take the seat that was in front of them, just as they had in the past.

"So you feel that you are ready to go alone." said the middle man.

"Yes sir. I have been there several times with my brother and Claudia. I feel that I'm ready.

Another man spoke. “Have you gone to them in their dreams?”

“No sir. I’m not sure how that is done”

The middleman spoke again. “If it’s ok with you we all agree that Claudia or your brother should go with you a few more times.”

The man at the end of the table spoke. “Yes, Claudia can now teach you to go to them in their dreams. Although we don’t think that souls should go a lot, but once in a while is nice.”

And with that, the middleman stood up and I was excused.

Walking out, my brother was waiting for me.

“How did it go?” he asked

“It was fine. They do want Claudia or you to go a couple of more times, to show me how to go to them in their dreams.”

“Great, I always enjoy showing the way and so does Claudia. Then it’s settled.”

Later that day I decided to walk out to Hanna’s. My brother was getting ready to go sailing. I am not sure what Claudia was doing.

Walking to Hanna’s was very nice. It gave me time to talk to God. Although I couldn’t see Him, I could feel Him and His love. I started to cry, not for sadness but for the joy of being in heaven and to know that God really does love me.

Getting ready to knock, Hanna’s opening the door

“Come in dear, how have you been?”

“Great and you? I asked.

Hanna chuckled “I’m in heaven.”

“Well you can’t get any better than that,” I said

“Come dear. Tell me everything you’ve been doing”

“Well where do I begin. Did you know that on top of the mountain you could see every planet known to man? And on the ocean, the stars are so bright and there are so many. Claudia said that a lot of the shooting stars are souls coming home.

“At night after everybody goes home, I like to walk to the mountain myself. It’s so beautiful. What else dear? Tell me everything.”

“I have also seen my children. We have a new baby. Her name is Roses. The first couple of times were strange. Next time I go I’m going to them in their dreams.”

“Besides the baby, what else is new? Has a lot changed?”

“No, I guess just life. They are living their lives. ~ Hanna your children are here. The man you married is here, what’s that like?”

“It’s great. I don’t make as many trips to earth. I wait until they come home and then welcome them into the family. After all heaven is where we all really want to be. But some time I would like to go with you and see your new granddaughter."

"I would love that." I said.

Hanna and I sat and visited about everything until her family started to come in. Well my family to. They all brought food and drinks.

"Hanna" I asked "is somebody coming home?"

"No dear, not today. We always gather at the end of the day before we go to church."

It was good to be here. The older ones and I mean the ones that have been here for a long time tell about the day they got here. They were all wonderful stories. You could feel the love that we all had for one another.

I met up with Claudia and my brother that evening at church

"Hi, how was your afternoon at Hanna's." Claudia asked

"It was great; a lot of the family came over."

"Everyday" Claudia said. "I don't know how Hanna's place got picked. But she loves it."

"Claudia. How about going to see the children in their dreams today? I asked eagerly.

Claudia looked at me oddly

"You know, to go see the children in their dreams "I explained.

"Ok. But just one at a time them having the same dreams well you know. Claudia giggled'. "They might seek a, what's the word I'm looking for, you know the people that talk to the dead. We are far from dead. For the first time its good to just tell them your fine. That you wanted to make sure they were ok as well, keep it short ".

"That's it?" I asked in a disappointing voice.

"Yes just for know. Sarah it won't be long and they will be at Hanna's with you, having fun with us. Don't worry they will be here when the Lord is done with them on earth."

"Your right "I said, really knowing that she was right. " So let's go."

Claudia started to laugh, "I think it would be better if we wait till they are asleep Sarah."

A little embarrassed of my eagerness, I agreed.

Claudia and I were still talking when my brother came walking out of the church with a very pretty girl. Long brown hair, slender, with a pinkish sundress on and one of them big floppy hats.

"Are we still going to supper?" my brother asked.

"Yes" Claudia said as she gave the girl a hug and asked how she had been.

"Great Claudia. It's good to see you again."

Then she turned to me as if we were old friends.

"Hi" as she gave me a hug," how are you?" She asked.

"Fine thank you, I said with a smile.

"You must be Sarah. Your brother told me you finally came home.

Are you enjoying heaven?"

I realized that everybody asked that question. As if this is a vacation and it will end. I agree it feels like a vacation, but I would cry if this ever ended.

"I'm sorry" my brother said "Sarah, this is a good friend of mine, Cindy."

"Hi. How are you?" I asked

"I'm great." Cindy said.

"We are taking it slow with Sarah. You know I enjoy every moment of showing off heaven."

"That's good. God says eternity. I love that my family took it slow with me. There is so much to see and do."

As we talked, we started to walk to get a bite to eat.

"Sarah" Cindy asked. "Have you been to see your children?"

"Yes Claudia has taken me several times. Tonight we are going to see them in their dreams. Well one of them tonight and then on another day I will go see the other one."

"Your new granddaughter is so cute. I love playing with them while they can still see us."

"You have seen her?" I asked

"Yes your brother and I go see everybody in his family and mine."

On the way to get something to eat Cindy, like Hanna and Claudia, also spoke to everybody along the way in such a caring manner.

"Did you know that your brother and Cindy are soul mates?" Claudia asked. Yes we are" my brother said and smiled warmly at Cindy. "We never met on earth. We both came home at an early age. But the first time I saw Cindy I knew. But of course we took it to the counselors."

"So do you get married or how does that work?" I asked

"Your brother feels the same way I do. Doing Gods work is really what matters to us.

"Helping all the children that come home. There is so much to do here." Cindy said.

"Yes Sarah. You remember how it was when you came home; you wanted to go see the children. Nobody really wants to go back, but the children do miss their mom and dad." Claudia explained.

"I really never thought of that. I think I understand." I said

My brother came over to me and said. "You will understand more after you have been here longer."

After we ate it was time to talk to one of my daughters.

"Are you ready Sarah to go see your daughter? I think we should see the oldest first. If that's ok with you".

"Yes that's fine. I'm so excited Claudia.~~~

We said our goodbyes and within moments we were standing in my daughter's bedroom.

"How do I do this Claudia?"

"Just talk to her. It will be as if she is dreaming."

When I started to talk to her, the whole room changed; all of a sudden, we were standing in a field of flowers.

"Mom is that you?"

At first, I was not sure and for some reason Claudia had disappeared. But I spoke anyway. Grabbing her hands, she started to cry.

"Don't cry sweetheart, its ok."

"Mom I miss you so much"

"Are you doing ok, I see you have had a little girl, she is so beautiful."

"Yes her name is Rosés."

"I know. I have to go; I just wanted to make sure you are doing fine"

"Yes mom I'm fine, are you doing ok?"

"Yes dear, now give me a hug"

And just like that, Claudia and I were standing beside her bed again. My daughter woke up, went to her living room, and started to cry.

"Mom I miss you so much. I wish you were here"

"Claudia I thought she would be happy, but she's crying."

"She is happy. But to her it was a dream. She does miss you. She doesn't realize that it was real. They really want it to be real," explained Claudia.

"So when can I go see the other daughter."

"Sarah we better give your oldest daughter some time, she will be telling the other one so probably a month or so."

We stayed there with my daughter until she went back to bed. Then it was time to head back to church. I cannot explain how church in heaven makes you feel, but it is the place to be and be near.

A month or so had gone by and it was time to go see the other daughter. I had not really bothered Claudia about it. Seeing my other daughter had not seemed to make her happy. I was a little nervous. But it was time. When I was on earth, if you got one daughter something then you had to get the other daughter something also. Therefore, it didn't seem right if I did not go back. So there we were standing over my other daughter.

"Go ahead Sarah talk to her, its fine." said Claudia. Trying to encourage me and reassure me.

"Hi dear, How are you?" I asked

Like the first time Claudia disappeared. Only this time we were standing in the streets of New York and people were coming and going.

"Hi momma."

"Hi dear, give me a hug, how are you?" I asked

"I'm fine momma. I miss you. I have so much to tell you, I really miss talking to you."

"Me too sweetheart, I have to go; I just came by to make sure you are fine."

"Yes, I'm fine." she said with a very peaceful smile. "Do come back momma sometime. We will talk," she said

"I will, but I have to go now. Come give me a hug."

As I was hugging her, like before, all of a sudden I was standing beside her bed again with Claudia.

"How did that go?" Claudia asked.

"Much better. She seemed to be very happy, even without me."

"You raised good strong women."

"But why is the oldest so sad? Well it seemed to make her sad." I said

"Because she is a mother and right now she is with child again. So she is a little emotional. But she didn't know when we were there."

"I see." was all I said. After being in heaven, I have realized we really do not miss anything. We can see our family when we want; it really is having the best of both worlds.

"Are you ready to head back?" Claudia said

As we headed back, Claudia wanted to show me something. I could not believe it. It was the moon.

"This never stops being exciting, does it Claudia?"

I never really got an answer since she was as much in awe as I was even though she had been here before. However, on the moon, you could see earth and all the planets that you could see in heaven. And here on the moon you could see heaven, and it was so bright that it lit up space so you could see everything. And even from a distance, heaven looked so peaceful.

"Claudia." I asked, "We can see heaven. But you cannot see it from earth or what about when they fly to the moon. They can't see it?"

"No they have to be like us, in spirit not in body. I love to come here, talk to God. When they do fly to the moon they have no idea how close they are to heaven. It's really amazing when you think about it."

"The wonders of heaven never stop do they?" I asked. "As long as you have been here you have never tired of it? Although, I could not see how anybody could."

"Tire of being this close to God, and all the wonders. Even if we didn't have all this, just being close to God would be enough."

I agreed with her. His glory is so powerful, it is the most love I have ever felt.

CHAPTER SEVEN THE REJOICE OF COMING HOME

Walking into church this morning, everybody was crying. There was a man at the altar that was preaching, he also had to stop to wipe away his tears.

I thought to myself, why is everybody crying, we're in heaven. And then the man started to speak again.

"We can only think we know what pain Jesus went through that day, the pain he suffered. He was thirty-three and scared; he asked God why and told Him he was frightened even if everybody in this room died a terrible death".

(The man stopped to wipe away more tears.)

"Our death could not amount to what Jesus felt that day, the day they hung Him on the cross. But before~! #!~. They beat sweet Jesus as He carried His own cross, then they laid Him down on that cross and the first nail went in His hand. He cried out in pain."

(Cry's came from the congregation)

"Then they put His feet together and nailed His feet together. Then they set the cross upright and waited for the son of God to die. Jesus asked as He hung on the cross. MY God why have you forsaken me...! ~!~! But God had not forsaken Jesus."

(The man stopped to wipe away more tears). "God could not bear to see His only begotten son die because Jesus died for us. He took all our sins on Him that day. He bore our sins, so we could be here today in heaven, just as God promised. So you see our death was a blessing. We got to enjoy a life on earth, and now we get to enjoy heaven forever."

The man raised his arms up to our Lord saying. "We worship you Lord. We honor you and there are no Gods before you."

I was crying myself and had not even realized it. I stood up also and raised my arms as far as I could to reach for our Lord thanking Him for my life on earth and in heaven, and special thanks for his son Jesus.

After Church, I wanted to talk to the man that was preaching today. I have always walked away with a great feeling from church, just being near God. But today was different. I know that we are in heaven because of Jesus, but I realized for the first time, and I already knew, but it hit me in this place, this wonderful place is all due to the blood of Jesus Christ.

As the man walked out, he was hugging people, shaking hands, so I made my way to the man.

"Hello." I said as I shook his hand, "I'm Sarah."

"Sarah". What a pretty name. I'm Jacob, but my friends call me J. Have we met Sarah? I feel as if maybe we knew each other on earth. "

"No I don't believe so."

"That's so funny I feel as if I know you," he said

He was a tall, very handsome man, jet-black hair, had an American Indian look about him.

"I wanted to tell you how much I enjoyed your preaching."

"Thank you. When you get up there, it's so easy to talk about God."

"Yes I can see that it would be."

"Have you ever been up there yourself Sarah?" he asked

"No I haven't been here that long. It's all new. I've seen a lot since I have been here. But there is so much."

"So have you been here long enough to show me heaven."

I was a little confused it was as if he has always been here.

"I have just arrived today," he said

"I would love to show you heaven. My friend Claudia and my brother Greg can also show you. They are still showing me. This place is amazing."

I took J to the restaurant to get lunch.

"So J you just got here today, but you seem to have been here for ever.

So sure of yourself and everything."

"I'm in heaven now Sarah. How sure do you have to be, this is the safest and most loved I have ever felt. And I had very loving people around me all the time on earth." he explained.

"I guess it was not that easy for me."

"I don't understand." he said

"Yes, I do not understand myself. Do you have children?" I asked.

"No. My wife and I never had children. How about you? Did you have children?"

"Yes, I had two daughters. I've been there to visit them a few times. I miss them, but I can go see them anytime I want. There is a lot going on in heaven, and they say this is the place to be, and everybody that says that is right. Later I will take you to the top of the mountain. We'll walk."

Unconcerned about the fact I said we would walk to the top of a mountain he simply asked how long it would take us.

After eating, we met up with Claudia, Greg, and his friend Cindy. J met everybody and we all headed for the mountain. The whole time everybody was explaining things to J. That everything was over the hill. And no matter where you were, you would always be in walking distance of our Lord.

On top of the mountain, J was so touched with the view that he fell to his knees thanking God. So we all went over and got on our knees and thanked God with him. I don't know if I was just a strange one, but seeing J's reaction to all of this, well I was kind of questioning my own home coming,

"Claudia." I asked, "J is taking this so well. I had a hard time, I do not understand."

Not understanding, I was worried, I love the LORD so much that I would die for Him a thousand times, and I would not trade my life in heaven, near my Lord for anything. So I was just really feeling that I've let the Lord down in someway.

"It's ok Sarah. All of this is so wonderful that it is hard to believe that it is all for us. God knows this. Heaven and earth are two very different places. I don't know what J left behind, but you have two kids. And now you know that getting their place ready in heaven is very important .Some people's lives may not have been as good as the next so when they are here, when they have finally come home, they know they are home. They have no wants about going back to see their loved ones. They will see them when they come to heaven. I think J is or was ready to come home."

J was listening to all this and explained that he had battled with cancer for several years. When his soul left his body he knew where he was going and why. That was what that powerful preaching he had done was all about. That God had promised all of this, but even if he had not had all this just being in the Lords presence was more than enough.

We all agreed. And the wonder of heaven was a plus. After we stayed on the mountain, we all headed back to church.

Over the next few weeks, we all showed J a lot of heaven; I took J to see the counselors. I think his went different from mine.

"How did that go?" I asked

"Great. They said I could get a place when I was ready, but I feel that I want to explore. So I think I will stay at Claudia's, that's what they suggested."

"Claudia says that people that don't want to get a place of their own stay with her, and her place is big enough. Very nice also."

I have just returned from seeing the higher counselors. This time was different from the rest. Walking in and sitting down they all greeted me as always.

"Sarah, how are you doing?

I'm fine, thank you. I'm going to help with the church play for Christmas. I've talked to the children."

"Good Sarah. We all agree that you are ready for your own place."

Another man spoke. "Yes do things on your own. We are very glad that you were so helpful to J."

"Yes" said the middleman again "We have also noticed that your trips to earth are not as much."

"No sirs. Heaven is where I want to be, it's hard to leave this wonderful place. So does this mean I cannot come see all of you anymore."

The middleman spoke "No, we encourage everybody to come see us whenever you feel like it. Please, always be our guest we are here to help and share in your joys."

"I see. That is very kind of all of you. You have all been very helpful to me, thank you."

The last man at the table spoke "Remember when we told you that soon you could get your own place, and to think about where you want to live."

Yes I remember and I've thought about it also. I want to stay near my brother so if it's all right with all of you I would like to have a place on the beach."

"Would you like to build this yourself or would you like us to have it ready for you?"

Thinking this was funny "Well I can't build it my self; I don't think I can anyway."

"Then we will prepare this for you."

The middleman stood and I was excused.

I headed back to church. Heaven has been an amazing place, and here there are no worries.

After church, there were five of us. Cindy, Claudia, J, my brother, and myself. We all had our things we do but at the end of a day we all get together at one of their places. Well J is still staying with Claudia. But tonight we all headed to Greg's place.

"We have a surprise for you." Greg said

"For me. What could it be?" I asked

About that time, we came over the hill and there was my brother's boat in the water but on the beach was the cutest little cottage, and it was mine.

"When did they do this?" I asked

"After you told them what you wanted. Come on lets go in." Claudia said with excitement.

Walking in the front door I was so in awe. "It's so pretty. Look at all this stuff."

I ran through the house looking at everything, then I went upstairs, there were two bedrooms up there; one was mine and the other was a guest room, the walls were done in flowered wallpaper, the bathroom was done in marble, so elegant, it was so nice.

"So, do we get a meal here?" My brother said. "I don't know. Do we have food here?" I said as I walked into the kitchen. I opened the cabinets and they were full of food and plenty of food in the refrigerator, and cold drinks

"Do they always do this?" I asked

"Unless you want to build it yourself, a lot of souls want to do that and while they are building they sleep outside under the stars." Cindy explained.

"I love to do that, I still sleep outside on the boat, its great, the peace and watching all the souls come home Greg said."

"Well I wanted to be near you and I love the ocean, so this is perfect. I might even take in guests when your place gets filled Claudia."

CHAPTER EIGHT
THE WALK OF A LIFE TIME

After church, Claudia asked me if I would come with her to see some of her friends. She said it would be one of the new things I haven't done. I had not made any other plans, and was up for the adventure.

I really cannot even image there is more to this wonderful place. ------ Claudia says I haven't even seen half of heaven.

"Today we will need the horses," Claudia explained

"Really, I thought everything was over the hill?" I asked in a joking tone.

"Well most things are. There are a few things in heaven that are a few hours away. And today is that day; we get to see a different way they live here in heaven.

"You know when we go to the top of the mountain. Today we are going down the other side." Said Claudia

"I see. That sounds very interesting."

I realize that no matter what we do. No matter how dangerous it would be on earth, there is no fear of doing anything here. God completely takes care of us. In return, all He wants from us is to live in peace and be happy. I want to do his work for Him. He has sacrificed so much for us.

When we got to the top of the mountain, we got off our horses to take in the view. Then we headed down the other side. We walked the horse's down for a while. It was a lot steeper than the side coming up. It didn't look like the trail had been taken much. Not much of a path. But it was really a lot of fun going down. New ground I had not explored. It was apparent that Claudia had been here a few times. She knew exactly where we were going. I could see that the mountains seemed to go on forever.

But in the middle of the mountains, it opened up onto a large field. There was a huge garden growing that we walked around --- to make sure that we didn't step on anything. Then we came to a forest that we walked through for a very short time and then it opened up. There was a waterfall, with a silvery river running.

"What is this place Claudia?"

"See the river? Do you remember the story about the babbling river? That is it. It thanks God for its existence.

I was speechless. We continued to ride a little bit more, when we came to a lot of little huts. There were not a lot of people around. Out of one of the huts came a beautiful girl. She had long jet-black hair. Dark skin. She was dressed as if she was going to a hula party in Hawaii. Looked to be in her early twenties. She came over and greeted Claudia in a language I didn't know, or had ever heard. Then she greeted me.

I love the fact that no matter where you are in heaven, everybody greets you in the same way. You are their family. I guess so. We are all Gods' children. We are on earth also but you don't have anything to fear here. Someday it will be like that there to. When God goes back to earth for his people.

"She invited us to go swimming in the river. They're all going." Said Claudia

"Who, all I see is a few people"I said.

As I was saying that I was looking around. Over by one of the huts came a very old man with a rug. He put the rug on the ground, and then sat down on it.

"Come on Sarah, Let's go. The water is so fresh and warm."

"I will be there in a minute,"I said.

I am not sure why that old man was so fascinating to me. He realized I was staring at him and motioned for me to come over and sit with him. I looked back and by that time Claudia and the rest of them were already in the water splashing and having a good time so I decided to go sit with him. We sat there for a long time watching everybody, when he got up and went inside his hut. He returned quickly with a book in his hand. He was trying to get me to hold the book. It looked very old. I was almost afraid that it would crumble in my hands. Without saying anything he assured me that it would be fine.

I took the book and looked at the old man that had sat back down. He wanted me to open it so I did and all of a sudden, we were not sitting beside the hut anymore. Everyone we were watching was gone except for the old man. He pointed in front of us. He was trying to show me something.

There was a man and a woman. The woman was pregnant. She looked like she was in pain. That's when I realized what this book was. Well I thought I knew what the book was. It turned out to be so much more!!!. This was Joe and Mary. The night Jesus was born.

We watched after Jesus was born. The three wise men came. It was happening just as it says. Only right before my eyes.!!! I went to the manger that he was laying in. I didn't know if they could see me or not. They didn't pay any mind to me. I did reach down and touch Jesus' hand. Even a few hours old. You could still feel the greatness.!!!!!

The old man came over and led me away. He wanted me to turn the pages. And just as quickly as we got there, we were gone.

This time there was a group of young people standing around. They were all laughing and having a good time.Thats when I realized who one of the young men was. It was Jesus in his early twenties. I started to go over, but the old man pulled me back and motioned for me to turn the page again. And we were gone again.

I was thinking that the next trip was to see Jesus hang on the cross. I was scared!!!!! I didn't think I could stand to see that. **Our forgiving Jesus**. The man that bore our sins! I looked at the old man, trying to let him know with my eyes that I was frightened to see that. He smiled and took the book and turned the pages himself.

Then we were back in heaven. This was the day Jesus got here and took his thrown beside our father (GOD)!!!!!.

The thrown was like something I have never seen. Not even in books. It was out of what looked like redwood, but not like I have ever seen before, it seemed to have the night stars in the wood; it was as if you could go pull the stars out. I'm not sure but it looked as if they were moving. The top of the back part of the chair, right above Jesus head was diamonds the size of a brick.!!! And they sparkled so much and had such a shine it was almost blinding. Huge armrests that had a beautiful design that was also covered in smooth diamonds the size of bricks...

There were people all around bringing him gifts. The gifts were not elegant. They were things of the heart.

I wanted to go myself, but I didn't have any thing to offer. The old man went up there and bowed before him, and kissed his hand. He turned to me to do the same. I don't really know if this is real, but touching him was.----- Then we were back beside the hut.

By the time, we had ended or journey together and shut the book every body was coming up from the river.

"You missed it. That's ok will go back after dark. The water sparkles and glows in the moon light." said Claudia.

I was still a little speechless, after all that was a journey I would not have ever even dreamed about. Heaven just gets better and better.

As we were getting ready to sit for a meal I noticed that people were coming from everywhere. From all four sides of the mountain. There was over a hundred now.

"Claudia, who are all these people?"

"They all live here. They were all out doing things."

We had a great meal. We sat on rugs out side. The rugs looked like a magic carpet. Only you couldn't fly with them. Well you might, I never tried.

After we ate, the old man that showed me the book stood up and started telling about his time in heaven. Not his time on earth. I still could not understand the language, so Claudia was telling me what he was saying.

"Claudia, what about when he was on earth?"

"He died about a week after Jesus came home. So you see that was some time ago. I'm sure he remembers it but why. He has lived in paradise for centuries. So of course, all his families are here. And have been. No reason to look back." Claudia explained.

"That explains the book," I said

"Yes. He was there the day Jesus died for us. He was given the book by Jesus when he came home. They said he stayed very faithful to Jesus. Even if it meant his and his family's death. And it did."

"I see" was all I said. It did make me look at the man in a different way. His dedication to Jesus was greater then his fear of dying. And now he gets the reward forever.

When the sun went down, they all dressed up in costumes and started to dance and sing around the fire.

"What's going on now Claudia? I asked

"They're dancing for God. They're showing him in their way how much they love him. There was even gifts brought that was put by the fire. Claudia even had a gift. And like before, I came with nothing.

"It's ok Sarah. This is from both of us."

I don't know what she gave; I was not able to see it with all the other gifts.

After the dance was over I think this was church for them. We all went swimming. The water really did glow. You could see the bottom. There was rocks on the bottom that was covered in gold. The light from the moon made them shine. It looked like there were lights on the bottom of the river.

When we got back up to the fire it was almost out. I realized that all the gifts were gone. I looked at the old man, and he just smiled.

The next day it was time to get back. I went over and thanked the man. I'm sure he could understand me. And I told him I would be back.

Our horses were already saddled and ready for us. We said goodbye to the rest of the people in the village and we were off.

CHAPTER NINE
GRANDMA'S ARRIVAL

Time has passed here. Everyday in heaven is truly a gift from God. I have been here for several months. Not sure. When you're in heaven time really doesn't matter. I met up with my grandpa and his brothers and parents today. My little group and myself.

"Hi grandpa. What is going on?"

Grandpa had a very excited look on his face and all the family was coming together again. When you have such a large family, and there is so much to do here and see, it's hard to get everybody in the same place at one time. I may have been the newest one of the family to come home. Nevertheless, I realized somebody else was coming home by everybody's excitement. I am not sure who it is but somebody is.

"Claudia what's going on? Is somebody coming home"? I asked.

Yes, it's your grandma. Look how excited your grandpa is and her parents are also here."

I never met her parents. They were not at the family reunion when I came home. At the time, I wasn't sure of anything so I never asked.We were all at the church waiting for her when all of a sudden the church doors open and their stood my grandma. She was not bent over from her back. She was standing tall; her fingers were not bent from arthritis. She looked like she did when she was in her 50s. She always looked very good then. My grandpa went to her and took her by the hand and led her to the front of the church where they both got on their hands and knees and started thanking God for their life together on earth and now in heaven.

After church we all gathered at Hanna's. I met my grandma's parents. I asked why I didn't meet them before. They said they had spent a while on earth with my grandma until she came home.

"Claudia is this the way we greet everybody when they come home?"

"Why do you ask Sarah?"

"Well, I was just thinking about it. It was different than mine."

I was feeling a little odd. When I came home, I stayed in the church for a while and then it was slowly that I met all the family. I was not sure of things. When J got here, he was so sure that there was not any thinking of his family. It was all about being here. I'm beginning to think my homecoming was not supposed to be yet.

"Sarah. I ask you, has God every let you down?" Claudia asked

"NO!!!!"

Then stop worrying, all I can tell you is that God has a plan. Don't worry Sarah you will find the answer in time."

I'm not real sure what she meant by that but my grandma came over about that time to talk to me.

"Come sit with me Sarah outside."

Her and I went outside in Hanna's back yard and sat on the swing that was made for two.

"Grandpa is very happy and your parents. That's so strange to meet everybody that had already come home; you know that were here before I got here."

"It's not so strange to me." Grandma said.

"Really Grandma, why is that?"

My grandma seemed to know more about this than I did. She has not even been here a day.

"Because Sarah this is what you're grandpa and I lived for our whole life? This is what we always told you and the rest of the children. The promise of God, do you understand?"

"I understand grandma. I have seen such beautiful things here. It's wonderful but I wonder about my homecoming, it seems to be different than everybody else's. Do you know why?" I asked,

"In time Sarah you will find the answer that you need. God will show you the way when He is ready for you to have the answer. In the meantime, I want you to enjoy heaven and the family. And don't forget a thing."

I looked at her as not to understand. She stood up and grabbed my hand, and we went back to the family.

"The next day my brother and I went out to see our grandparents. Their home was so nice. My grandpa built it with his own hands. He had everything ready for grandma.

"HELLO." My brother yelled." Is anybody home?"

"Yes, come in." They both said at the same time and then giggled about it.

"We are going to the ocean today and grandpa says you have a boat Greg."

"Yes I do. I would love to show you the ocean. We can go out so far that you can't see land and go swimming.

"I would love that. Your grandpa says we can swim with all the fish."

"It's wonderful out on the boat. I stayed out there till I got my own place." I said

"I heard you have your own place. That's great Sara; I can't wait to see it."

They asked us to join them for breakfast and to go with them before we go on the boat.

"Where are you guys going?

"To see the counselors. They want to talk to your grandma. They always welcome everybody that come home, talk to them and see how they are, ask if there is anything else they want. I can't even think that anybody would want more. I really don't think anybody has asked for more things. Maybe a job to give back to God what he has given to us."

"I see, kind of like the man at the hotel that works in the restaurant. Hanna said he was there because he wanted to be there but we might not see him there again I said

"Yes that's right. Cindy and I help with all the children that come home." Greg said

"Right know I'm helping a man build a house. He said when he was on earth he could never do that but with Gods help it can be done. Therefore, I am helping with that. And there are things your grandma and I want to do together for God."

Walking to the church before we went to see the counselors it surprised me that my grandma was greeting people she had never seen before and they all welcomed her home.

My grandma got up to play the piano in church. They always have an orchestra play. It was always such beautiful music. However, grandma had not been able to play for many years and she missed it. After playing a while, the orchestra joined in. Several of the women got up and sang to God. It was such sweet music.

When we got to what I call the old courthouse Grandma went in by herself. Then they sent somebody else out to get my grandpa. I had never seen anybody else in that room besides the five men and there were no doors there except for the one we went in to enter. So I don't know where that person came from.

Greg is there another door in there?"

"I don't know. Why?"

"No reason. I wonder why they wanted both of them in there."

"Because they were married they were lucky. They spent their young life, their middle age and their old age together and were always happy. They always put God before themselves and when hard times did come it went in Gods hands." Greg explained.

About that time, they both walked out.

"Are you both ready? I'm excited to get out in the ocean" Grandma said.

Out on the boat we all went swimming when we got out far enough. I have to admit I really wanted to ask what was said when they both went in but they never offered so I never asked.

After a long swim, we sat and ate and talked about everything under the stars.We told her about going to the moon. All the cool things in heaven to see.

Have you all been to the jungle? There is a waterfall. A bunch of us always go up there and jump off the cliff into the water" grandpa explained.

"I've been there. It's a lot of fun. It is a big jump. Its like you are flying and then you hit the refreshing water." explained Greg

"I've been there to. We haven't taken Sarah there. Maybe we should all do that tomorrow."

Looking around to see who was talking Claudia came climbing on board. That was strange since we were miles and miles away from shore. "Claudia" I said, "What are you doing? You swam all the way out here. I am so sorry. I was not sure where you were when we left."

I had not done many things without her. I felt badly about leaving her.

"Don't feel bad Sarah you needed some time with your grandparents."

Claudia greeted everybody and she started telling my grandparents what we have done, since I have been home. We stayed on the boat all night watching the stars and explaining that the shooting stars were souls coming home. I think grandma was just as amazed as I was. On earth, we can only think we know what heaven holds for us. However, when we get here, it is more than we could ever even dream about.

The next day a very large group of us went to the waterfall. They were all taking turns. And one by one they all jumped over the cliff .There were only a few of us left on top. One of them was my grandma. She looked at me and said it was her turn and she jumped. I followed. It was great. They were right; it was as if you were flying before you hit the water.

We all stayed so long that we decided there were so many of us we would hold church right here and as soon as one of the men stood up and started telling about what God has done for him animals started coming out of the jungle. There were animals I had never seen on earth. So I raised my hand as if I was in school. The man that was talking asked me if I had a question or did I want to get up and tell the group all the wonders of heaven.

"No, I have a question. As soon as you started talking about God they all came out?"

"That's right. God created them also and has given them a good life here in heaven so they are like us. Very eager to hear about are savoir also."

"I understand that but some of these animals I have never seen before."

"That's because they lived their life to the fullest and with so many changes on earth could not survive on earth any longer."

And with that he continued to preach.

CHAPTER TEN
WALKING WITH JESUS

"Good morning Hanna, I wanted to come visit you."

I see her all the time in church but I never get to catch up on what has been going on,

"Remember when I asked you what it was like to have your family all home?" I asked

"I remember dear, it's wonderful."

"Having my grandma home is great. And someday the children will be here. So I had the privilege of raising them and know I will get to show them heaven. When I first got here, everybody said there was a lot to do and I see now we're always getting ready for family and friends to come home."

Hanna was getting a basket of fruit ready as if she was going somewhere.

"Come out back with me dear, I need to pick a few more apples, I'm going to walk this over to one of our friend's house. Would you like to come along?"

"No Hanna if it's all the same to you I would love to just sit here for awhile."

"Stay as long as you like I will be back dear."

And with that, Hanna left. I stayed there for a while just loving everything that God has done for us when all of a sudden a warm bright light started to shine out of the forest. The light was so bright and warm that you could feel the love from it. I decided to go in the forest and find where this light was coming from. I was way in the forest and the love I felt was getting so strong that I started to cry. Then I came to the end of the forest.

There was a man sitting on a big rock. I knew who it was. It was Jesus. I fell to my knees at his feet crying, thanking him for everything. He took my arm to lift me. I could never explain in a million years what its like to be in the presence of such greatness and love.

Jesus had a long whiter than white robe on. Shoulder length, brown hair. His eyes glimmered, even in the shade. I knew where they got the word peace from. It was from Him, just looking at Him you could feel and see the peace on His face and through His touch.

We walked back in the forest until we got to Hanna's and then he left, and I knew at that moment I had to go back for a short time.

I woke up in a hospital bed with all my family around me before I opened my eyes, I could hear my girls talking.

"Should we tell her that her grandma passed away a couple of days ago?" The oldest asked.

"No, she doesn't need to hear that. It might make things worse."

"Girls, please come here."

"Mom, your awake we are so scared mamma!!!!!" the youngest said.

"I know. It's going to be ok. I tried to reassure them.

I asked my oldest daughter to come closer.

"It's all right. I want you to know that the next baby you have will be a girl. And you will have a very good husband.

"Mamma, do you know that I met a man that wants to marry me and take care of us?"

"Yes." I could feel my body getting heaver ~-~ I realized that I didn't have much more time before I finally go home.

"Please girls come closer." I asked

As the girls came closer, they were crying I felt so bad. OR I felt bad about being excited about going to heaven.

"What mamma, what can we do for you?" they asked

"It's alright. I have seen heaven and have walked with Jesus. I'm going home. I will get things ready for you and the families you will have.

Trying to reassure them, I could feel the life in my body leaving.

"And for you" As I turned my head to look at the youngest daughter, "You will also be fine. Keep working for God. He will take you as far as you want to go."

Both of the girls were holding each other's hands across my bed. Then they started to pray. They were praying that I have a safe trip home and at that moment my soul left my body.

As my soul started floating, I could see myself laying there, my body lifeless. A nurse came in and checked to make sure that I was gone. Then she put the sheet over my face and I knew it was over, and I was really going home.

When I got to the church, there was not a soul around. The view was just as it was before. I was so thankful to be here, back in heaven. Only this time I would never have to leave again.

It was a little strange that nobody was around. Before there was always people coming and going. I started to get a little worried that I had not died and was still in my body; that I was just dreaming about heaven. Then I remembered, I decided to open the church doors and go in .When I opened them, there was all my family~~~ they were waiting for me, just as we all did for my grandma.

Claudia came over and took me by the hand to lead me to the altar.

"Is this for real" I asked her "or am I dreaming again?" "No Sarah, this is real we have been waiting for you." Standing at the altar was my brother, J, and Cindy. I looked over to the right of me and there were both of my grandparents, clapping with joy along with the rest of the family. The rest of the church joined in, welcoming me home.

I stood at the altar and got on my knees and I started to pray. "Dear father, thank you for the life you have given me on earth. Thank you for the gift of my children and grandchildren. Thank you for all my lessons and the ability to teach my children about life and how wonderful you are and thank you dear LORD for my death so that I can be a part of heaven and closer to you." I understand. I know the answer that everybody was saying that God would show me when the time was right.

I am very thankful that I got a glimpse of heaven before coming home and now I will get things ready for my children.

THE BEGINNING

Printed in the United Kingdom
by Lightning Source UK Ltd.
117304UKS00001B/388